C000132532

THIS ANNUAL BELONGS TO...

Name:	Age:

Favourite player:

2022/2023

My Predictions...	Actual...

Leeds United's final position:

Leeds United's top scorer:

Premier League winners:

Premier League top scorer:

FA Cup winners:

EFL Cup winners:

Contributors: Peter Rogers, Andy Greeves

A TWOCAN PUBLICATION

©2022. Published by twocan under licence from Leeds United Football Club.

Every effort has been made to ensure the accuracy of information within this publication but the publishers cannot be held responsible for any errors or omissions. Views expressed are those of the authors and do not necessarily represent those of the publishers or the football club. All rights reserved.

ISBN: 978-1-914588-72-3

PICTURE CREDITS:
Leeds United Football Club, Action Images, Alamy and Press Association.

£10

CONTENTS

HEAD COACH

JESSE MARSCH

Jesse Marsch became Leeds United's new Head Coach in the second half of the 2021/22 season, replacing the popular Marcelo Bielsa. The former USA international midfielder, who previously played for DC United, Chicago Fire and Chivas USA in the MLS, helped turn around Leeds United's faltering campaign. Four wins, three draws and just three defeats (to Manchester City, Arsenal and Chelsea) in their last ten Premier League matches of the season saw Leeds United maintain their Premier League status.

Marsch's men also got off to a good start to the 2022/23 Premier League campaign, with results including a 2-1 home victory over Wolverhampton Wanderers on the opening weekend and a 3-0 win over Chelsea at Elland Road on 21 August 2022.

Marsch retired from playing back in 2009, bringing to an end a career which had seen him score 31 goals in 321 MLS appearances for his three different clubs. He also won two caps for his country, featuring as a substitute in a goalless draw with Trinidad and Tobago in a FIFA World Cup qualifier in November 2001 and almost six years later in a 4-1 friendly win against China in San Jose, California in June 2007.

He became an assistant coach to then United States manager Bob Bradley in 2010, before being named as the first head coach of Montreal Impact in 2012. Three years later, he was named New York Red Bulls boss and led them to the MLS Supporters' Shield as he was named 2015 MLS Coach of the Year.

Marsch joined German Bundesliga side RB Leipzig as assistant to Ralf Rangnick in 2018 before being named head coach of sister club Red Bull Salzburg ahead of the 2019/20 season. He went on to enjoy great success in Austria, winning both the Austrian Bundesliga and Austrian Cup in consecutive seasons in 2019/20 and 2020/21. That success led to him returning to RB Leipzig as Head Coach in the summer of 2021.

Marsch signed a three-year contract to become Leeds United's Head Coach on 28 February 2022. In doing so, he became the third American to manage in the Premier League, after Bob Bradley and German-born David Wagner.

NUMBER OF SEASONS WITH LEEDS UNITED:

11

LEEDS UNITED APPEARANCES:

256

LEEDS UNITED GOALS:

3

PLAYER OF THE SEASON WINNER:

1997/98

LEGEND

LUCAS RADEBE

LEEDS UNITED ACHIEVEMENTS: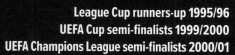

League Cup runners-up 1995/96
UEFA Cup semi-finalists 1999/2000
UEFA Champions League semi-finalists 2000/01

MAJOR STRENGTH:

Strong and composed, Radebe was an unflappable central defender who read the game perfectly

INTERNATIONAL ACTION:

Radebe won 70 caps for South Africa between 1992 and 2003 and was part of the Bafana Bafana side that won their first-ever African Cup of Nations in 1996. He was also part of their squad for both the 1998 and 2002 FIFA World Cups

FINEST HOUR:

On an official visit to Leeds in 2001 to become an honorary freeman of the city, former South African president Nelson Mandela described Radebe as his 'hero'

Two defensive stalwarts, Gary Kelly and Lucas Radebe were regular starters in ultra-competitive Leeds United teams of the 1990s and 2000s.

Right-back Kelly is the only player in Leeds United history from outside of the Don Revie era to make more than 500 appearances for the club and has more Premier League appearances for Leeds - 325 - than any other player.

A winner of a PFA Special Merit Award for his contribution to football in 2010, Radebe is fondly referred to as 'The Chief' at Elland Road. He played 197 of his 256 appearances for the club in the Premier League, and is widely acknowledged as one of the finest centre-backs in the club's history,

Both are undisputed Whites' legends, but who was the best?

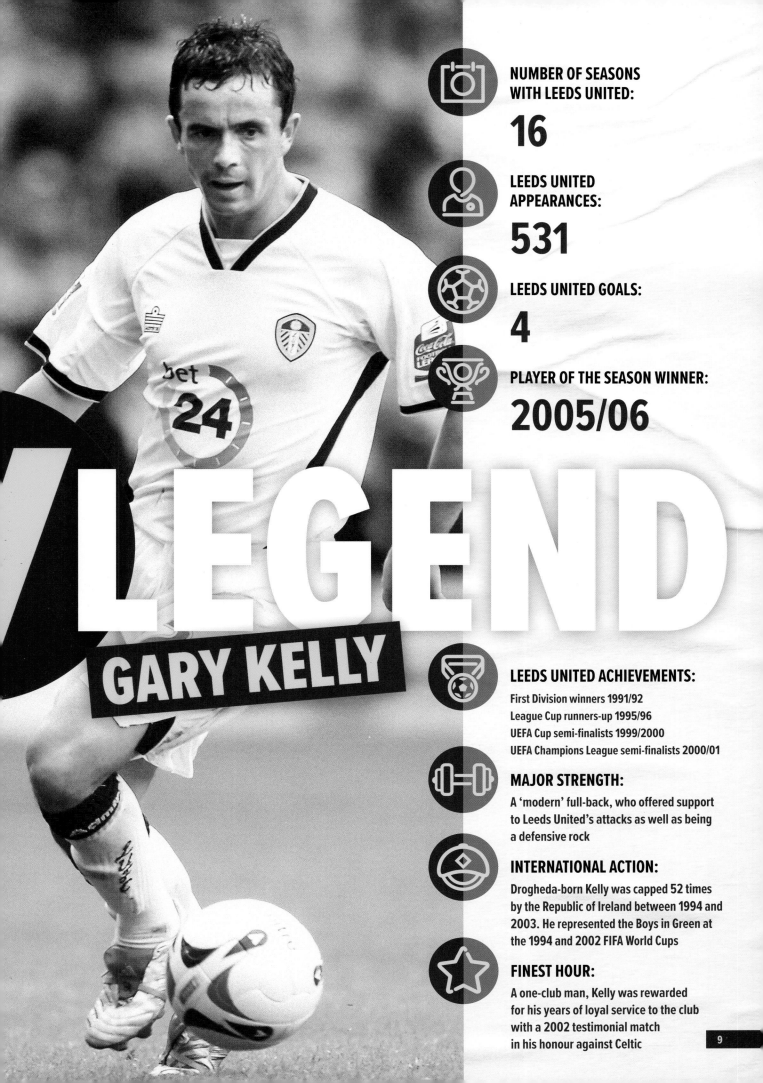

LEGEND
GARY KELLY

NUMBER OF SEASONS WITH LEEDS UNITED:

16

LEEDS UNITED APPEARANCES:

531

LEEDS UNITED GOALS:

4

PLAYER OF THE SEASON WINNER:

2005/06

LEEDS UNITED ACHIEVEMENTS:

First Division winners 1991/92
League Cup runners-up 1995/96
UEFA Cup semi-finalists 1999/2000
UEFA Champions League semi-finalists 2000/01

MAJOR STRENGTH:

A 'modern' full-back, who offered support to Leeds United's attacks as well as being a defensive rock

INTERNATIONAL ACTION:

Drogheda-born Kelly was capped 52 times by the Republic of Ireland between 1994 and 2003. He represented the Boys in Green at the 1994 and 2002 FIFA World Cups

FINEST HOUR:

A one-club man, Kelly was rewarded for his years of loyal service to the club with a 2002 testimonial match in his honour against Celtic

Defending is not just about stopping the attackers and clearing your lines. Making the best of possession you have just won is vital - although the danger has to be cleared, it is important for your team to keep hold of the ball.

FOOTBALL SKILLS
LONG PASSES

When passing your way out of defence, and short, side-foot passes are not possible, the longer pass, driven over the heads of midfield players, can be used.

EXERCISE

In an area 40m x 10m, A1 and A2 try to pass accurately to each other, with a defender B, in the middle between them. Player B must attempt to stop the pass if possible, and A1 and A2, must keep the ball within the area of the grids.

After each successful long pass, the end player will exchange a shorter pass with B before passing long again, thus keeping the exercise realistic and also keeping the defender in the middle involved. The player in the middle should be changed every few minutes, and a 'count' of successful passes made for each player.

KEY FACTORS

1 Approach at an angle.
2 Non-kicking foot placed next to the ball.
3 Eye on the ball.
4 Strike underneath the ball & follow through.

Practice is the key to striking a consistently accurate long pass and to developing the timing and power required.

The same end result could be achieved by bending the pass around the defender instead of over him, and this pass could be practised in the same exercise, by striking the football on its outer edge (instead of underneath) which will impart the spin required to make the ball 'bend' around the defender - not an easy skill!

PREMIER LEAGUE 2022/2023 SQUAD

1 ILLAN MESLIER
GOALKEEPER DOB: 02/03/2000 COUNTRY: FRANCE

Ever-present in Leeds United's 2021/22 Premier League campaign, Illan Meslier has firmly established himself as the club's first choice goalkeeper following his 2019 arrival from Lorient.

The 22-year-old Frenchman made a number of vital saves as the club successfully maintained top-flight status last season and the 'keeper was once again one of the first names on head coach Jesse Marsch's teamsheet as the 2022/23 campaign began.

2 LUKE AYLING
DEFENDER DOB: 25/08/1991 COUNTRY: ENGLAND

Now one of the longest-serving players at Elland Road, the 2022/23 campaign will be defender Luke Ayling's seventh season with Leeds United.

As popular as ever with the club's supporters and highly respected by his teammates, the 31-year-old full-back has now amassed over 200 league games for Leeds United having initially joined the club from Bristol City back in 2016.

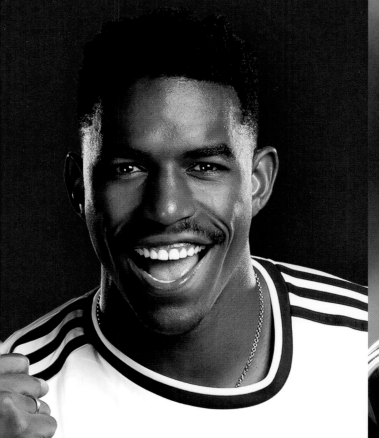

 3 **JUNIOR FIRPO**
DEFENDER   DOB: 22/08/1996   COUNTRY: SPAIN

4 **ADAM FORSHAW**
MIDFIELDER   DOB: 08/10/1991   COUNTRY: ENGLAND

Versatile defender Junior Firpo made 24 Premier League appearances for Leeds United last season following a summer 2021 move from Barcelona to Elland Road.

The former Spain U21 international full-back began his career with Real Betis, before joining Barcelona in August 2019. He was a Copa Del Rey winner in 2020/21.

All at Elland Road were delighted to see 30-year-old midfielder Adam Forshaw finally put his injury-plagued spell behind him by returning to first-team action last season.

Playing in the August 2021 EFL Cup tie against Crewe Alexandra was Forshaw's first taste of senior action in almost two years. He went on to make 22 Premier League appearances and in January 2022 he agreed a new contract with the club.

5 ROBIN KOCH

DEFENDER DOB: 17/07/1996 COUNTRY: GERMANY

The new 2022/23 Premier League campaign signals defender Robin Koch's third season at Elland Road having joined the club from Bundesliga club SC Freiburg in August 2020.

An accomplished ball playing central defender, Koch enjoyed 20 Premier League outings last season and having figured heavily in head coach Jesse Marsch's plans in the early weeks of the new season, he should soon have amassed half a century of games for the club.

6 LIAM COOPER

DEFENDER DOB: 30/08/1991 COUNTRY: SCOTLAND

A vastly-experienced campaigner, central defender and club captain, Liam Cooper brings a wealth of knowledge and knowhow to Leeds United's defensive unit.

The Scotland international was just four appearances away from reaching the 250 mark as the new 2022/23 season began. A bargain £600,000 signing from Chesterfield in 2014, Cooper is now in his ninth season at Elland Road.

7 BRENDEN AARONSON

MIDFIELDER   **DOB: 22/10/2000**   **COUNTRY: USA**

Attacking midfielder Brenden Aaronson joined Leeds United from Red Bull Salzburg in July 2022.

A full USA international, Aaronson made his Leeds United debut on the opening weekend of the 2022/23 Premier League season as Leeds began with a 2-1 home victory over Wolverhampton Wanderers. The American was then the toast of Elland Road when he netted his first goal for the club to open the scoring in the 3-0 demolition of Chelsea on 21 August.

8 MARC ROCA

MIDFIELDER   **DOB: 26/11/1996**   **COUNTRY: SPAIN**

Spanish midfielder Marc Roca joined Leeds United from German giants Bayern Munich in June 2022. The 25-year-old central midfielder began his career in his homeland with Espanyol before moving on to Munich in 2020.

His Leeds United career got off to a winning start as Wolverhampton Wanderers were beaten 2-1 on his Elland Road debut. Across the opening month of the new season he quickly established himself as a regular starter in Jesse Marsch's team.

9 PATRICK BAMFORD

FORWARD DOB: 05/09/1993 COUNTRY: ENGLAND

Leeds United's go-to man for goals in recent seasons, forward Patrick Bamford suffered an injury ravaged 2021/22 season. The 29-year-old forward, who can operate anywhere across the front line, will be hopeful of an injury-free 2022/23 season when he can once again become a regular starter and consistent goalscorer in Leeds colours.

With one England cap to his name, Bamford will be aiming to get back amongst the goals and propel himself into contention for England's 2022 FIFA World Cup finals squad.

10 CRYSENCIO SUMMERVILLE

MIDFIELDER DOB: 30/10/2001 COUNTRY: NETHERLANDS

Dutch U21 international winger Crysencio Summerville joined Leeds United from Feyenoord in September 2020.

Patience was the key as he waited twelve months for his first taste of Premier League action which arrived when he replaced Raphinha in Leeds United's 1-1 draw with Newcastle United at St James' Park in September 2021. He made a further eight first team appearances last season and made his first start of the current campaign in the 3-1 EFL Cup victory over Barnsley.

PREMIER LEAGUE
2022/2023
SQUAD

11 JACK HARRISON

MIDFIELDER DOB: 20/11/1996 COUNTRY: ENGLAND

Having spent three seasons on loan with Leeds United from Manchester City, midfielder Jack Harrison put pen to paper on a permanent deal at Elland Road in July 2021.

As a full-time Leeds United player, Harrison enjoyed an exceptional 2021/22 campaign which included a memorable hat-trick in the Whites' 3-2 Premier League victory over West Ham United at the London Stadium in January 2022. He also netted the dramatic late winner in the final day victory over Brentford as the club secured Premier League status for 2022/23.

12 TYLER ADAMS

MIDFIELDER DOB: 14/02/1999 COUNTRY: USA

Midfielder Tyler Adams became the second USA international to arrive at Elland Road in the summer of 2022 after Brenden Aaronson.

An experienced USA international with 30 international appearances to his name, Adams was previously with New York Red Bulls before joining Leipzig in January 2019. The 23-year-old was one of many new faces to be handed his Leeds United debut in the opening-day victory over Wolverhampton Wanderers at Elland Road.

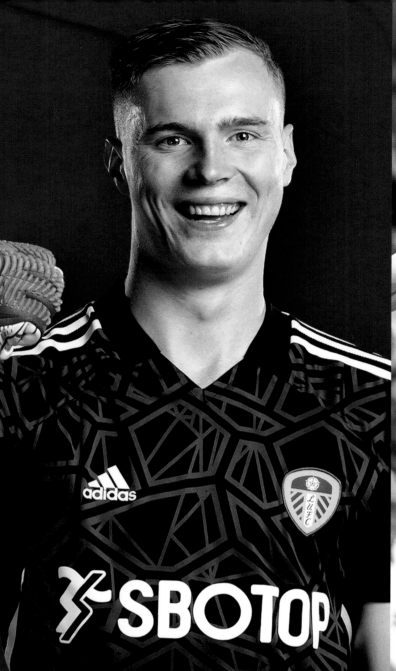

13 KRISTOFFER KLAESSON

GOALKEEPER   DOB: 27/11/2000   COUNTRY: NORWAY

Norwegian U21 international goalkeeper Kristoffer Klaesson arrived at Elland Road in July 2021 from Valerenga.

With Illan Meslier sidelined with injury, Klaesson's Leeds United debut arrived in March 2022 against Wolverhampton Wanderers as Leeds United edged a five-goal thriller 3-2 at Molineux. The Oslo-born stopper continues to provide cover and competition in the club's goalkeeping department.

14 DIEGO LLORENTE

DEFENDER   DOB: 16/08/1993   COUNTRY: SPAIN

Composed Spanish international defender Diego Llorente has been a regular face in the Leeds United side ever since his 2020 signing from Real Sociedad.

The 29-year-old defender chipped in with three Premier League goals last season, the first of which gave Leeds United a vital 1-0 Elland Road victory over newly-promoted Watford in October 2021. Highly-rated by head coach Jesse Marsch, Llorente featured in the all of the club's Premier League fixtures in the opening month of the current campaign.

15 STUART DALLAS

MIDFIELDER   **DOB: 19/04/1991**   **COUNTRY: N IRELAND**

Northern Ireland international Stuart Dallas has made over 250 appearances for the club.

He featured in every Premier League game for the Whites during the 2021/22 season until April, where he unfortunately suffered a leg fracture against Manchester City. The 2022/23 season will be Dallas' eighth at Elland Road and he is continuing his long road to recovery.

18 DARKO GYABI

MIDFIELDER   **DOB: 18/02/2004**   **COUNTRY: ENGLAND**

Leeds United completed the signing of teenage midfielder Darko Gyabi from fellow Premier League side Manchester City.

The highly-promising central midfielder began his career with the Millwall Academy before moving north and helping Manchester City's U18s land the Premier League north title in 2022/21. The powerful 18-year-old agreed a four-year deal at Elland Road.

19 RODRIGO MORENO

FORWARD   **DOB:** 06/03/1991   **COUNTRY:** SPAIN

Spain international forward Rodrigo netted six Premier League goals as Leeds United battled to maintain their top-flight status in 2021/22.

The 31-year-old former Valencia man started the current campaign in exceptional form for Jesse Marsch's side with four goals in his opening three league appearances including a brace in the 2-2 Elland Road draw with Southampton.

21 PASCAL STRUIJK

DEFENDER DOB: 11/08/1999 COUNTRY: NETHERLANDS

It was defender Pascal Struijk who netted the all-important last-gasp equaliser against Brighton & Hove Albion at Elland Road in the final home game of last season to secure a 1-1 draw as the team fought to maintain their top-flight status.

After joining the Whites from Ajax in January 2018, Struijk had to be patient in his pursuit of matchday action at Elland Road but is now seen as a first-team regular.

22 JOEL ROBLES

GOALKEEPER DOB: 17/06/1990 COUNTRY: SPAIN

Spanish stopper Joel Robles completes the goalkeeping structure at Elland Road having joined the club as a free agent following the expiry of his contract with Real Betis in July 2022.

The 32-year-old custodian is no stranger to the English game having previously played for Wigan Athletic, where he was an FA Cup winner in 2013, and more recently Everton.

23 LUIS SINSTERRA

MIDFIELDER DOB: 17/06/1999 COUNTRY: COLOMBIA

Colombian international winger Luis Sinsterra joined Leeds United in July 2022. Signed from Dutch club Feyenoord, where he had netted 20 goals in 76 league appearances, his transfer to West Yorkshire is believed to have been Feyenoord's record transfer sale.

The exciting 23-year-old looks set to become a firm favourite at Elland Road and netted his first goal for Leeds in the 3-1 EFL Cup victory over Barnsley in August.

25 RASMUS KRISTENSEN

DEFENDER DOB: 11/07/1997 COUNTRY: DENMARK

Another new face at Elland Road for 2022/23, right-back Rasmus Kristensen was added to Jesse Marsch's squad in June 2022 following a transfer from Red Bull Salzburg.

A full Denmark international with eight caps for his country, 25-year-old Kristensen made his Premier League debut in Leeds' opening game of the current season when Wolverhampton Wanderers were defeated 2-1 at Elland Road.

29 WILFRIED GNONTO

FORWARD **DOB:** 05/11/2003 **COUNTRY:** ITALY

Italian international forward Wilfried Gnonto joined Leeds United on the final day of the 2022 summer transfer window when he completed a switch from Swiss Super League champions FC Zurich.

A product of Inter Milan's Academy, Gnonto spent eight years with the San Siro outfit before moving to Zurich in 2020. The highly-rated teenager agreed a five-year deal at Elland Road, running until the summer of 2027.

30 JOE GELHARDT

FORWARD **DOB:** 04/05/2002 **COUNTRY:** ENGLAND

Young forward Joe Gelhardt picked the perfect moment to score his first Elland Road goal, netting the most dramatic of last-gasp winners to secure three priceless Premier League points from a 2-1 victory over Norwich City in March 2022.

A strong and robust front-man, Gelhardt possesses great close control and dribbling skills. An England U20 international, he joined Leeds United in August 2020 from Wigan Athletic.

33 LEO HJELDE

DEFENDER **DOB:** 26/08/2003 **COUNTRY:** NORWAY

Leeds United swooped to sign Norway U21 international defender Leo Hjelde from Celtic in August 2021. The 6ft 2in defender made his Leeds United debut in January 2022 in an FA Cup third round match against West Ham United.

His Premier League debut arrived a week later, also against the Hammers, when he became the youngest Norwegian to play in the Premier League.

37 CODY DRAMEH

DEFENDER   **DOB: 08/12/2001**   **COUNTRY: ENGLAND**

Dulwich-born Cody Drameh began his youth career with Fulham before making the switch to Leeds United. The defender stepped up from the U23 development squad last season and made his first-team debut in an EFL Cup tie with Arsenal in October 2021.

A first Premier League appearance came against Norwich City later that month before the England U21 international joined Cardiff City on loan in January 2022. He impressed greatly at the Cardiff City stadium and was voted the Bluebirds' Young Player of the Season for 2021/22.

42 SAM GREENWOOD

FORWARD   **DOB: 26/01/2002**   **COUNTRY: ENGLAND**

England youth international Sam Greenwood joined Leeds United from Arsenal in the summer of 2020.

He went on to make his Premier League debut against the Gunners in December 2021. In total, Greenwood enjoyed nine first-team outings last season and has again continued to feature for the Whites this season under Jesse Marsch.

43 MATEUSZ KLICH

MIDFIELDER   DOB: 13/06/1990   COUNTRY: POLAND

Experienced Polish international midfielder Mateusz Klich is closing in on 200 appearances for Leeds United having joined the Whites from FC Twente in the summer of 2017.

He played a vital part in the club's 2019/20 Championship title-winning campaign and scored the first Elland Road goal of last season in the 2-2 draw with Everton. The 32-year-old midfielder grabbed his first goals of 2022/23 when he scored twice in the EFL Cup victory over Barnsley in August.

63 ARCHIE GRAY

MIDFIELDER   DOB: 12/03/2006   COUNTRY: ENGLAND

The 16-year-old is one of the latest players to come through the ranks at Thorp Arch.

He featured on the bench for Leeds United six times last season and was also included in the club's pre-season tour of Australia ahead of the 2022/23 campaign. He is the great nephew of Leeds United legend Eddie Gray, grandson of Frank Gray and son of Andy Gray, who all played for the Whites.

MULTIPLE CHOICE

Here are ten Multiple Choice questions to challenge your footy knowledge!

Good luck...

ANSWERS ON PAGE 62

2. Which company produce the current Leeds United playing kit?

A) Nike B) Puma C) Adidas

3. Raphinha was Leeds United's top Premier League scorer last season. How many goals did he score?

A) 11 B) 12 C) 13

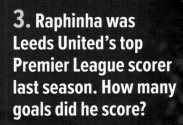

1. Who has squad number 11 at Elland Road for 2022/23?

A) Stuart Dallas
B) Jack Harrison
C) Tyler Adams

4. What nationality is defender Pascal Struijk?

A) Swiss
B) Dutch
C) Swedish

5. Against which club did Leeds begin their 2022/23 Premier League campaign?

A) Arsenal
B) Leicester City
C) Wolves

6. At which venue did Leeds secure their first away point of the 2022/23 Premier League season?

A) St Marys B) Anfield
C) Old Trafford

7. What is Adam Forshaw's middle name?

A) James
B) John
C) Joel

10. When Leeds United won the Championship title in 2019/20, how many points did they end the campaign with?

A) 91 points
B) 92 points
C) 93 points

8. Who did Leeds defeat in the second round of the 2022/23 EFL Cup?

A) Bolton Wanderers
B) Barnsley
C) Bradford City

9. On how many occasions have Leeds United been English top-flight champions?

A) Twice B) Three times
C) Four times

MARC ROCA

ANSWERS ON PAGE 62

FAN
TASTIC

Lucas the Kop Cat is hiding in the crowd in five different places as Leeds United fans celebrate victory over Chelsea in August 2022.
Can you find all five?

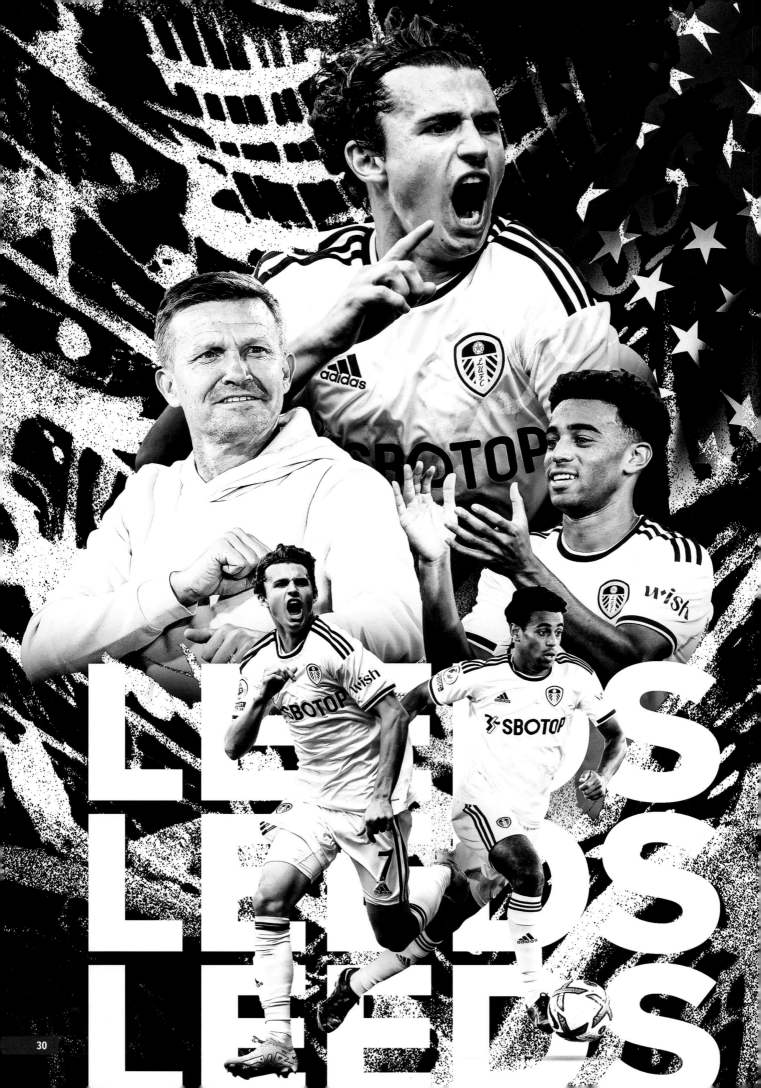

LEEDS LEEDS LEEDS

Close control in tight situations creates havoc in opposition defences - particularly when receiving the ball in the air - and nine times out of ten, when a striker receives the ball, he has his back to goal.

FOOTBALL SKILLS
RECEIVING THE BALL

Quite often the ball will arrive in the air, and good strikers have to be able to cope with that - controlling and turning in one movement, ready for the instant shot.

EXERCISE 1

In an area 20m x 10m, two players A and A2 test the man in the middle, B, by initially throwing the ball at him in the air, with the instruction to turn and play in to the end man - if possible using only two touches.

The middle player is changed regularly, and to make things more realistic, the end players progress to chipping the ball into the middle.

The middle player is asked to receive and turn using chest, thigh, or instep.

KEY FACTORS

1   Assess flight early - get in position.
2   Cushion the ball.
3   Be half turned as you receive.

EXERCISE 2

A progression of this exercise is the following, where the ball is chipped or driven in to the striker from varying positions. He has to receive with his back to goal, and using just two touches in total if possible, shoot past the keeper into the goal!

To make this even more difficult, a defender can be brought in eventually. For younger children, the 'servers' should throw the ball to ensure consistent quality.

TRAIN TO WIN

Making sure that you are fit, healthy and fully prepared is key to success in whatever challenge you are taking on. Those three factors are certainly vital for professional footballers and also for any young aspiring player who plays for his or her school or local football team. The importance of fitness, health and preparation are key factors behind the work that goes into preparing the Leeds United players to perform at their maximum on matchday.

The Leeds United players will need to demonstrate peak levels of fitness if they want to feature in Jesse Marsch's team. Before anyone can think of pulling on a smart white shirt and stepping out at Elland Road, they will have had to perform well at Thorp Arch to have shown the manager, his coaches and fitness staff that they are fully fit and ready for the physical challenges that await them on a matchday.

Regardless of whether training takes place at the training ground or at the stadium, the players' fitness remains an all-important factor. Of course time spent practicing training drills and playing small-sided games will help a player's fitness but there is lots of work undertaken just to ensure maximum levels of fitness are reached.

Away from the training pitches the players will spend a great deal of time in the gymnasium partaking in their own personal work-outs. Bikes, treadmills and weights will all form part of helping the players reach and maintain a top level of fitness.

Over the course of a week the players will take part in many warm-up and aerobic sessions and even complete yoga and pilates classes to help with core strength and general fitness. The strength and conditioning coaches at the club work tirelessly to do all they can to make sure that the players you see in action are at their physical peak come kick-off.

While the manager and his staff will select the team and agree the tactics, analysts will provide the players and staff with details on the opposition's strengths, weaknesses and their likely approach to the match.

Suffice to say the training ground is a busy place and no stone is left unturned in preparation for the big match!

NEW BOYS

The summer of 2022 was a busy one for Leeds United, with nine of new players signing for the Club.

Red Bull Salzburg pair Brenden Aaronson and Rasmus Kristensen were the first of Head Coach Jesse Marsch's summer 2022 signings. United States international Aaronson, who came through the ranks with MLS side Philadelphia Union, was handed the Whites' number 7 shirt. Danish right-back Kristensen previously turned out for Midtjylland and was an Eredivisie champion with Ajax in 2018/19 as well as collecting three Austrian Bundesliga and three Austrian Cup winners' with Red Bull Salzburg between 2019 and 2022. Aaronson shared in four of Kristensen's six successes.

Former Spanish U21 international midfielder Marc Roca was next to join the Marsch revolution at Elland Road as he arrived from Bayern Munich on a four-year contract. A two-time Bundesliga winner and a FIFA Club World Cup champion in 2020, Roca won the Segunda Division title with his first senior club, Espanyol, in 2020/21.

Tyler Adams instantly made himself at home at Elland Road, playing in Leeds United's opening six matches of the 2022/23 Premier League following a July 2022 move from RB Leipzig, where he had played UEFA Champions League football. The New York-born midfielder began his professional career with his local club, New York Red Bulls.

Colombian international winger Luis Sinisterra also made an instant impression in the famous white shirt, netting three times in six appearances in all competitions for Leeds United at the start of the 2022/23 campaign after joining from Feyenoord. With an on eye of the future, promising youngster Darko Gyabi was also signed by the club from Manchester City, as was forward Sonny Perkins from West Ham United. Experienced goalkeeper Joel Robles was brought in provide cover and offer competition to Illan Meslier and Kristoffer Klaesson for the Leeds United number 1 shirt following his move from Real Betis.

Leeds United's summer 2022 transfer window activity was completed with the singing of Italian international forward Wilfried Gnonto from FC Zürich. Born in Verbania, Italy, the forward was a member of Inter Milan's academy between 2012 and 2020 while he was a Swiss Super League winner during his time at Zürich and is Italy's youngest ever international goal scorer.

DREAM TEAM

Pick your ultimate Leeds United
dream team and design them a kit!

 RODRIGO
MORENO

PREMIER LEAGUE
DANGER MEN

20 TOP-FLIGHT STARS TO WATCH OUT FOR DURING 2022/23...

ARSENAL
GABRIEL JESUS

The Gunners completed the signing of Brazilian international striker Gabriel Jesus from Premier League champions Manchester City in July 2022.

A real penalty box predator, Jesus netted 95 goals in 236 appearances in a trophy-laden spell for City and Arsenal will be hopeful he can continue his impressive goals-to-games ratio at the Emirates Stadium.

ASTON VILLA
EMI BUENDIA

Now in his second season at Villa Park, following a big money move from Norwich City, a great deal will be expected of Argentinean international midfielder Emi Buendia in 2022/23.

A highly skilful and creative player, Buendia has the ability to create chances for teammates and score vital goals himself.

BOURNEMOUTH
KIEFFER MOORE

Giant front man Kieffer Moore chipped in with four goals in three games to help Bournemouth secure promotion to the Premier League last season.

The former Cardiff City man will be keen to prove his worth at Premier League level in 2022/23 in order to cement his place in Wales' squad for the 2022 FIFA World Cup finals in Qatar.

BRENTFORD
KEANE LEWIS-POTTER

England under-21 star Keane Lewis-Potter enjoyed an exceptional Championship campaign with Hull City in 2021/22 and that prompted Brentford to spend a club record fee to bring the exciting 21-year-old to West London.

A true attacker who can operate off of either flank, Lewis-Potter will be relishing the challenge of showcasing his skills at Premier League level.

BRIGHTON & HA
LEANDRO TROSSARD

After weighing in with eight Premier League goals last season, Belgian international winger Trossard has widely become recognised as the Seagulls' main creative force.

Hugging the left touchline and cutting inside to play in a teammate or striking for goal himself, Trossard is another player who will be looking to feature in the forthcoming World Cup.

CRYSTAL PALACE
WILFRIED ZAHA

Players may come and go at Selhurst Park, but the constant threat offered by the Crystal Palace club legend Wilfried Zaha remains firmly in place.

An exciting forward who loves to take opponents on in one-on-one situations, Zaha has now amassed over 400 appearances for the club across his two spells at Selhurst Park, and will be looking to fly the Eagles into the top half of the Premier League table.

CHELSEA
MASON MOUNT

Having progressed through the academy system at Stamford Bridge, attacking midfielder Mason Mount has become one of the first names on both the Chelsea and England teamsheet.

Mount hit eleven Premier League goals last season and boss Graham Potter will be keen to see more of the same as Chelsea look to put pressure on Liverpool and Manchester City in 2022/23.

EVERTON
JORDAN PICKFORD

Firmly established as first choice keeper for club and country, Jordan has been a reliable last line of defence for the Toffees since joining the club in summer 2017.

A host of match-saving games last season were rewarded with the Player of the Season award and the England No.1 has now played over 200 games for Everton.

FULHAM
ALEKSANDAR MITROVIC

Having fired home a record-breaking 43 Championship goals for Fulham in their title-winning campaign last season, all eyes will be on Aleksandar Mitrovic in 2022/23.

If Fulham are to shake off their yo-yo club tag, then the top-flight goalscoring form of their powerful Serbian striker is going to be key.

LIVERPOOL
MOHAMED SALAH

Together with goalkeeper Alisson and inspirational defender Virgil van Dijk, Liverpool forward Mo Salah has been the catalyst for the Reds' success in recent seasons.

The Egyptian superstar jointly topped the Premier League scoring charts with Spurs' Son Heung-min last season as Liverpool enjoyed a domestic cup double.

LEEDS UNITED
PATRICK BAMFORD

After suffering an injury-hit 2021/22, Leeds United striker Patrick Bamford will be hopeful that 2022/23 offers him the chance to demonstrate the form that won him a first full England cap in September 2021.

A versatile front man who can play as a lone striker or in a pair, Bamford can also operate as an attacking midfielder from either flank.

LEICESTER CITY
JAMIE VARDY

The goalscoring hero of Leicester City's sensational 2014/15 Premier League title triumph, striker Jamie Vardy once again topped the Foxes' scoring charts last season.

An energetic forward, full of running, Jamie never gives defenders a moment of peace, and will once again be the one to watch for goals at King Power Stadium in 2022/23.

MANCHESTER CITY
ERLING HAALAND

Manchester City pulled off the biggest summer transfer coup when they lured Norwegian striker Erling Haaland from Borussia Dortmund to the Etihad Stadium for 2022/23.

Boasting a phenomenal strike rate at Dortmund and with his national team too, Haaland is sure to bring goals galore to the Premier League champions.

MANCHESTER UNITED
BRUNO FERNANDES

Attacking midfielder Bruno has become the heartbeat of the Red Devils' forward play since signing from Sporting Lisbon.

Blessed with a wide range of passing skills, the 28-year-old Portuguese international has the knack of unlocking even the tightest of defences.

TOTTENHAM HOTSPUR
SON HEUNG-MIN

South Korean superstar Son ended the 2021/22 season by picking up the Premier League Golden Boot as joint top goalscorer along with Liverpool's Mohamed Salah.

Forming an almost telepathic partnership with England captain Harry Kane, Tottenham Hotspur will certainly be a team to watch if Son repeats his lethal form in front of goal again in 2022/23.

NEWCASTLE UNITED
BRUNO GUIMARAES

After joining the Magpies from Lyon in January 2022, Brazilian midfielder Bruno has become a real cult hero with the fans at St James' Park.

Bruno scored five Premier League goals in 17 games last season and looks set to be one of the first names on Eddie Howe's teamsheet in 22/23.

WEST HAM UNITED
JARROD BOWEN

Blessed with the ability to operate in a variety of attacking positions, Jarrod Bowen enjoyed an exceptional 2021/22 campaign.

The 25-year-old netted 18 goals in all competitions and made 51 appearances as the Hammers enjoyed a top-half finish and reached the semi-finals of the Europa League. He was also handed an England debut in June 2022.

NOTTINGHAM FOREST
DEAN HENDERSON

Forest made a real statement of intent following their promotion to the Premier League when they completed the season-long loan signing of the Man United keeper.

Capped by England, Dean will hope his City Ground performances can push him into England boss Gareth Southgate's thoughts for the 2022 FIFA World Cup finals in Qatar.

WOLVES
GONCALO GUEDES

Wanderers boosted their attacking options when they completed the signing of Portugal forward Goncalo Guedes from Valencia at the start of the 2022/23 season.

Capped on over 30 occasions by Portugal, the 25-year-old is well known to Wolves' boss Bruno Lage having played for him at Benfica earlier in his career.

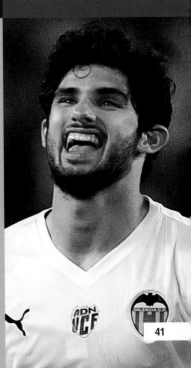

SOUTHAMPTON
JAMES WARD-PROWSE

One of the very best dead ball deliverers, Saints skipper Ward-Prowse has progressed through the academy ranks at St Mary's to play over 350 first-team games for the club.

James is another England star who will hope to be on the plane for Qatar 2022.

TRUE OR FALSE?

Here are ten fun footy True or False teasers for you to tackle! Good luck...

ANSWERS ON PAGE 62

2. Leeds United last won the FA Cup in 1972

3. Head coach Jesse Marsch was previously in charge of RB Leipzig

1. Harry Kane played four games on loan for Leeds United from Spurs

4. Patrick Bamford was signed from Middlesbrough

5. Liam Cooper wears Leeds United squad number five

6. Teenage forward Wilfried Gnonto has already played senior international football with Italy

7. Archie Gray is the grandson of Leeds United legend Eddie Gray

8. Jesse Marsch has previously managed the US national team

9. Leeds United signed full-back Luke Ayling from Bristol Rovers

10. In the 2021/22 season, goalkeeper Illan Meslier was Leeds United's only ever-present player

43

NUMBER OF SEASONS
WITH LEEDS UNITED:

5

LEEDS UNITED
LEAGUE APPEARANCES:

174

LEEDS UNITED LEAGUE GOALS:

80

LEGEND

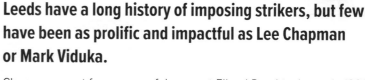

LEE CHAPMAN

LEEDS UNITED ACHIEVEMENTS:

Second Division winners 1989/90
First Division winners 1991/92
FA Charity Shield winners 1992

MAJOR STRENGTH:

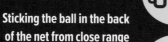

Sticking the ball in the back
of the net from close range

INTERNATIONAL ACTION:

While Chapman never represented his country at
senior level, he did earn one England U21 cap in
1981, and an England B cap a decade later

FINEST HOUR:

Scoring a hat-trick in a 6-1 away win
against Sheffield Wednesday as Leeds
won the final edition of the First Division
in 1991/92 before it was rebranded
as the Premier League

Leeds have a long history of imposing strikers, but few have been as prolific and impactful as Lee Chapman or Mark Viduka.

Chapman spent four successful years at Elland Road in the early 1990s, before re-signing on loan later on in his career. Australian international Viduka spent four seasons at the club, following a stunning spell of goalscoring north of the border for Celtic.

It's hard to split them - but let's at least try...

LEGEND
MARK VIDUKA

NUMBER OF SEASONS WITH LEEDS UNITED:

4

LEEDS UNITED LEAGUE APPEARANCES:

166

LEEDS UNITED LEAGUE GOALS:

72

LEEDS UNITED ACHIEVEMENTS:

Leeds United top season goalscorer 2000/01, 2001/02, 2002/03 & 2003/04

MAJOR STRENGTH:

Powerful finishes with the outside of his boot, into the corner

INTERNATIONAL ACTION:

He could also have played for Croatia or Ukraine, but Viduka opted for Australia and scored eleven goals in 43 caps for the Socceroos between 1996 and 2007. He represented Australia at both the World Cup and the Olympic Games

FINEST HOUR:

Scoring four Premier League goals against Liverpool in a 4-3 victory at Elland Road.

STAR SEARCH

ALL THE SURNAMES FROM THE LEEDS UNITED PREMIER LEAGUE SQUAD ARE HIDDEN IN THE GRID, EXCEPT FOR ONE... CAN YOU WORK OUT WHICH ONE?

```
W C W N R Y M D O O W N E E R G E Y R M
V E L L O R E N T E R I T H L M R K E O
B C A O K T U Y E Q U R U G B T E I J R
L W S R X H N O S N O R A A J L I F C E
V J G R A Y F I E S P T R S Z A R O O N
S W A O B M U S A F I R P O K X O R P O
T Z N C A D D K D F E C V O D P U S T Q
R G H A L S T J L T G W D H E Y L H N Y
U O C P G A U F S I P I J R F K Y A L U
I V I B E Q W N O E C S K A S O F W G H
J S R F N E I H E O J H E M A R D U O I
K D K R I S T E N S E N V S P I Z S P I
A J O F O G A N R Q I O R J A N A G T S
D T C D N B A T M G T D R A H L E G J K
I L H M G H L M M I H L Y A X O L B F D
Y F U G N U Z E P X I S D R O F M A B D
X V C C I O U K S O B P U L H E K F D G
S M E S L I E R I B A L P F U P C E K N
A S V W Y E O Z C Y Y M J V B P W J B H
X C B V A N L B K K G N O N T O L N M M
```

MESLIER	AARONSON	MORENO	GELHARDT
AYLING	ROCA	STRUIJK	HJELDE
FIRPO	BAMFORD	ROBLES	DRAMEH
FORSHAW	LLORENTE	SINSTERRA	GREENWOOD
KOCH	DALLAS	KRISTENSEN	KLICH
COOPER	GYABI	GNONTO	GRAY

46

ANSWERS ON PAGE 62

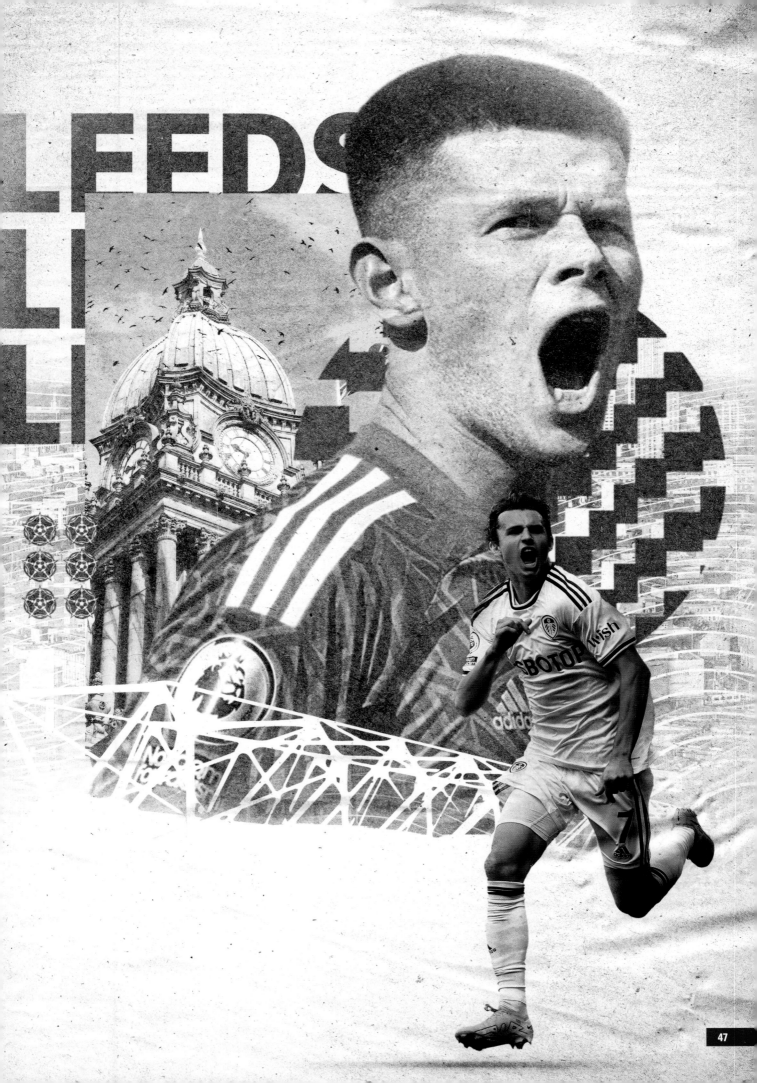

LEEDS

WHICH BALL?

Can you work out which is the actual match ball in these two action pics?

48

ANSWERS ON PAGE 62

SPOT THE DIFFERENCE?

Can you spot the eight differences between these two photographs?

Once the 2022 FIFA World Cup finals in Qatar are finalised, Leeds United will be straight back into the cut and thrust of Premier League action when champions Manchester City visit Elland Road on Boxing Day. The calendar year of 2023 certainly has some exciting and challenging fixtures on the agenda. Here are six big games for the Whites in 2023.

NEW YEAR
SIX PACK

WEST HAM UNITED
HOME · JANUARY 2023

The New Year kicks off at Elland Road with the visit of last season's Europa League semi-finalists West Ham United.

Almost twelve months on from Jack Harrison's superb hat-trick in our thrilling 3-2 victory at the London Stadium last season, a similar match would certainly make for an eventful start to 2022. Our two Premier League fixtures with West Ham last season produced a total of eight goals and this match looks set to be another entertaining affair.

MANCHESTER UNITED
HOME · FEBRUARY 2023

One of the most eagerly-awaited fixtures on the Leeds United calendar sees Manchester United provide the opposition on 11 February.

Leeds will go in search of a first Elland Road victory over the Red Devils since the 1-0 Premier League win in September 2002. Last season's clash served up six goals and this game is once again all set to be another mouth-watering Elland Road event.

CHELSEA
AWAY · MARCH 2023

Having turned on the style in the August sunshine to record a highly impressive 3-0 Elland Road victory over Chelsea earlier this season, Jesse Marsch's men will head to Stamford Bridge in March searching for a Premier League double over the Londoners.

Victory at Stamford Bridge would be Leeds' first win there since a Stephen McPhail brace secured a 2-0 triumph in December 1999, while our last league double over Chelsea dates back to the 1991/92 First Division title-winning campaign.

LIVERPOOL
HOME · APRIL 2023

There are never any easy games in the Premier League and they certainly don't get much tougher than going head-to-head with Liverpool.

The Anfield club will visit Elland Road on 15 April for a match that Leeds United will certainly relish. In 2019/20, following our return to the Premier League, we pushed Liverpool all the way in both fixtures and with Jesse Marsch's attacking approach to games, Leeds will certainly be aiming for all three points against the Reds in mid-April.

NEWCASTLE UNITED
HOME · MAY 2023

Leeds United's penultimate home game of the 2022/23 Premier League campaign sees big spending Newcastle United roll into Elland Road in May for what has all the makings of a must-see encounter.

With both sides embracing an attacking approach to games, there is bound to be end-to-end entertainment as the 2022/23 season reaches its climax. A repeat of our 5-2 thrashing of Newcastle at Elland Road in December 2020 will do just fine!

TOTTENHAM HOTSPUR
HOME · MAY 2023

Leeds United's storming end to the 2020/21 season saw a 3-1 victory over Tottenham Hotspur in May 2021 - a match that triggered a four-game winning run at the end of the season.

This season our visit from Spurs and England captain Harry Kane will bring the curtain down on another season at Elland Road. Spurs play an attractive brand of possession based attacking football - this really should be the classic encounter ahead of the summer break.

1. WHO AM I?

2. WHO AM I?

3. WHO AM I?

4. WHO AM I?

WHO ARE YER?

Can you figure out who each of these Leeds United stars is?

ANSWERS ON PAGE 62

5. WHO AM I?

6. WHO AM I?

7. WHO AM I?

8. WHO AM I?

53

LUIS SINI STE RRA

TRUE COLOURS

Can you colour
in this picture
of Jack Harrison?

55

PREMIER LEAGUE

FAST FORWARD>>

CHAMPIONSHIP WINNERS

CHAMPIONSHIP RUNNERS-UP

CHAMPIONSHIP TOP SCORER

PREMIER LEAGUE CHAMPIONS

PREMIER LEAGUE RUNNERS-UP

PREMIER LEAGUE TOP SCORER

THE CHAMPIONSHIP

THE FA CUP

FA CUP WINNERS

FA CUP RUNNERS-UP

FA CUP WINNING GOAL SCORER

LEAGUE CUP WINNERS

LEAGUE CUP RUNNERS-UP

LEAGUE CUP WINNING GOAL SCORER

THE LEAGUE CUP

**NUMBER OF SEASONS
WITH LEEDS UNITED:**

7

**LEEDS UNITED
LEAGUE APPEARANCES:**

235

LEEDS UNITED LEAGUE GOALS:

44

PLAYER OF THE SEASON WINNER:

1992/93

LEGEND

GORDON STRACHAN

Though very different players, Strachan and McAllister both became Leeds legends from midfield.

Both members of the Peacocks' title-winning class of 1991/92, Strachan was a wily and intelligent right winger, while McAllister was a tough-tackling yet attack-minded central midfielder. Both ex-Scotland internationals with over 50 caps each, this is a tough one to call.

But which was the better player?

LEEDS UNITED ACHIEVEMENTS:

First Division winners 1991/92
Second Division winners 1989/90
FA Charity Shield winners 1992

MAJOR STRENGTH:

Strachan had incredible ability with the ball between his feet, able to beat a full-back with ease - before crossing into the box

INTERNATIONAL ACTION:

Strachan earned 50 caps and scored five goals for Scotland and won Man of the Match in a 5-2 win over New Zealand at the 1982 FIFA World Cup, before scoring against West Germany at the World Cup in Mexico four years later. Between 2013 and 2017, he enjoyed a five-year tenure as Scotland manager

FINEST HOUR:

At the end of an outstanding season in 1990/91, Strachan won Football Writers' Association (FWA) Footballer of the Year, becoming the first player to win the award in both Scotland and England

NUMBER OF SEASONS WITH LEEDS UNITED:

6

LEEDS UNITED LEAGUE APPEARANCES:

294

LEEDS UNITED LEAGUE GOALS:

45

PLAYER OF THE SEASON WINNER:

1993/94

LEGEND

GARY McALLISTER

LEEDS UNITED ACHIEVEMENTS:

First Division winners 1991/92
FA Charity Shield winners 1992

MAJOR STRENGTH:

Rotating play and moving Leeds from defence to attack with smart, swift passes

INTERNATIONAL ACTION:

McAllister earned 57 Scotland caps in an international career which spanned nine years. He scored in a 3-0 win over CIS at UEFA Euro 1992

FINEST HOUR:

Scoring memorable goals against Stuttgart and Celtic during Leeds' UEFA Champions League run in the 1992/93 season

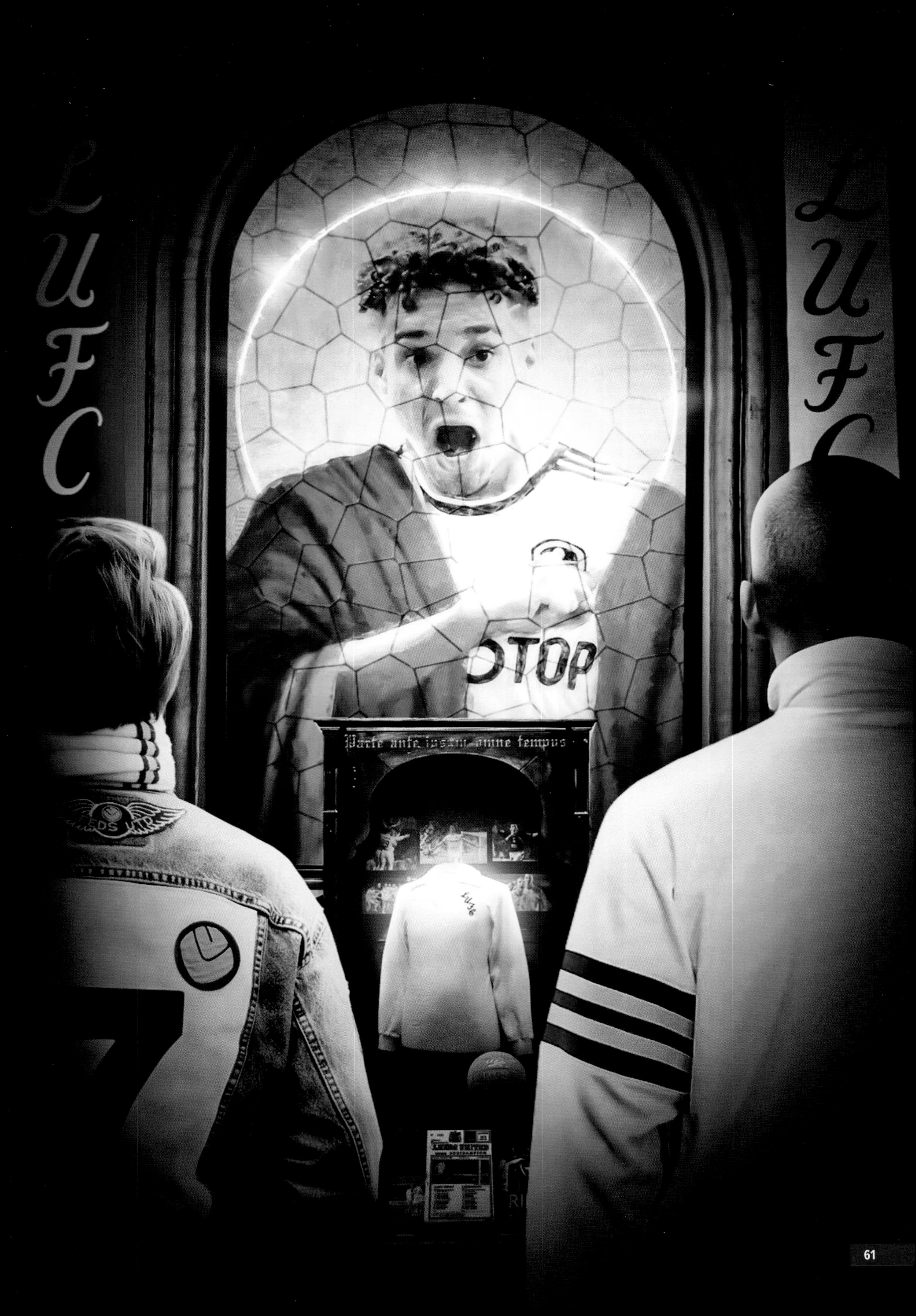
LUFC
OTOP

ANSWERS

PAGE 26 · MULTIPLE CHOICE

1. B. **2.** C. **3.** A. **4.** B. **5.** C. **6.** A. **7.** B. **8.** B. **9.** B. **10.** C.

PAGE 28 · FANTASTIC

PAGE 43 · TRUE OR FALSE?

1. False (Harry never played on loan for Leeds United).
2. True. **3.** True. **4.** True. **5.** False (Liam Cooper is squad
number six). **6.** True. **7.** False (Archie is Eddie's great-nephew).
8. False. **9.** False (he was signed from Bristol City). **10.** True.

PAGE 46 · STAR SEARCH

Hjelde.

PAGE 48 · WHICH BALL?

PAGE 49 · SPOT THE DIFFERENCE?

PAGE 52 · WHO ARE YER?

1. Tyler Adams. **2.** Robin Koch. **3.** Jack Harrison.
4. Pascal Struijk. **5.** Sam Greenwood. **6.** Archie Gray.
7. Marc Roca. **8.** Patrick Bamford.